KU-101-674

Aberdeenshire

3175099

ABERDEENSHIRE LIBRARIES	
3175099	
Bertrams	28/09/2015
J910.916	£11.99

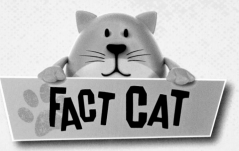

FACT CAT

SEAS AND OCEANS

Izzi Howell

WAYLAND

Get your paws on this fantastic new mega-series from Wayland!

Join our Fact Cat on a journey of fun learning about every subject under the sun!

First published in Great Britain in 2015 by Wayland
Copyright © Wayland 2015

All rights reserved
ISBN: 978 0 7502 9028 9
Library ebook ISBN: 978 0 7502 9029 6
Dewey Number: 910.9'162-dc23
10 9 8 7 6 5 4 3 2 1

MIX
Paper from
responsible sources
FSC® C104740

Wayland
An imprint of Hachette Children's Group
Part of Hodder & Stoughton
Carmelite House
50 Victoria Embankment
London EC4Y 0DZ

An Hachette UK Company
www.hachette.co.uk
www.hachettechildrens.co.uk

A catalogue for this title is available from the British Library
Printed and bound in China

Produced for Wayland by
White-Thomson Publishing Ltd
www.wtpub.co.uk
+44 (0) 843 208 7460

Editor: Izzi Howell
Design: Rocket Design (East Anglia) Ltd
Fact Cat illustrations: Shutterstock/Julien Troneur
Other illustrations: Stefan Chabluk
Consultant: Kate Ruttle

Picture and illustration credits:
NASA: Reto Stöckli, Robert Simmon, MODIS Land Group; MODIS Science Data Support Team; MODIS Atmosphere Group; MODIS Ocean Group, USGS EROS Data Center, USGS Terrestrial Remote Sensing Flagstaff Field Center, Defense Meteorological Satellite Program 4; Science Photo Library: Dante Fenolio 13, Tom McHugh 17; Shutterstock: Konrad Mostert cover, ian woolcock title page, Anna Jedynak 6, eFesenko 8, Thomas Klee 9, Tatiana Mihaliova 10b, trubavin 11, Leonardo Gonzalez 12, Pete Niesen 14, slava296 15, Juancat 16, Jaromir Urbanek 18, withGod 20, think4photop 21; Stefan Chabluk 5, 7; Thinkstock: Digoarpi 10t, jon666 19.

Every effort has been made to clear copyright. Should there be any inadvertent omission, please apply to the publisher for rectification.

The author, Izzi Howell, is a writer and editor specialising in children's educational publishing.

The consultant, Kate Ruttle, is a literacy expert and SENCO, and teaches in Suffolk.

FACT CAT FACT

There is a question for you to answer on each spread in this book. You can check your answers on page 24.

CONTENTS

WHAT IS AN OCEAN?

Nearly three-quarters of the Earth's **surface** is covered by water. Most of the water on Earth is **salt water**, found in seas and oceans. The rest is **fresh water**, found in lakes and rivers.

This picture of Earth was taken from space. From far away, we can see how much water there is on Earth. The blue is the water and the white is clouds.

North America

Arctic Ocean

Europe

Asia

Atlantic Ocean

Africa

Pacific Ocean

equator

South America

Pacific Ocean

Indian Ocean

Australasia and Oceania

Southern Ocean

Antarctica

An ocean is a large area of salt water. All of the salt water on Earth is connected, but we think of it as five different oceans.

The five oceans on Earth are called the Arctic Ocean, the Atlantic Ocean, the Indian Ocean, the Pacific Ocean and the Southern Ocean. Look at the map and find out which ocean is furthest north.

FACT CAT FACT

Each litre of water in the ocean contains 0.000000013 grams of gold. Across all the world's oceans, this adds up to around 20 **million** tonnes of gold!

WHAT IS A SEA?

A sea is a part of an ocean. Every ocean contains several seas. Seas are usually close to land.

The Caribbean Sea is part of the Atlantic Ocean. Look at the map on the next page – can you find the Caribbean Sea?

There are more than one hundred seas on Earth. Most of them are in the Pacific Ocean and the Atlantic Ocean.

This map shows some of the seas on Earth. Not all seas have the word 'sea' in their name. Look at the map and find an example.

Arctic Ocean

Greenland Sea

Barents Sea

East Siberian Sea

Norwegian Sea

Gulf of Alaska

Hudson Bay

Labrador Sea

Irish Sea

North Sea

Celtic Sea

English Channel

Bering Sea

Gulf of Mexico

Atlantic Ocean

Mediterranean Sea

Yellow Sea

Sea of Japan

Pacific Ocean

Caribbean Sea

Red Sea

Arabian Sea

Bay of Bengal

South China Sea

Philippine Sea

equator

Gulf of Guinea

Pacific Ocean

Indian Ocean

Timor Sea

Coral Sea

Tasman Sea

Scotia Sea

Southern Ocean

FACT CAT FACT

The water in the Yellow Sea is actually yellow! Its colour comes from sand and clay in the water.

COASTLINES

A coastline is the area where an ocean or a sea meets the land. Some coastlines have beaches made up of sand or **pebbles**.

Some coastlines have tall **cliffs**. These rocky cliffs are on the Atlantic coast of Portugal.

FACT CAT FACT

The total length of all the coastlines on Earth is 312,000 kilometres. Find out which country has the longest coastline.

Waves and wind move sand and pebbles along the coastline. This can **damage** the **habitat** of the animals and plants that live on the beach.

Small fences called groynes help to keep sand and pebbles in place.

groyne

WAVES

Waves are made when wind moves across the surface of the ocean. Most waves form in the middle of the ocean, and then move towards land.

These small waves are in the middle of the ocean.

Waves **break** when they reach **shallow** water near the coastline.

The size of a wave depends on the strength of the wind. Tall waves are good for watersports, such as surfing. Always ask an adult before going into rough water, because it can be dangerous.

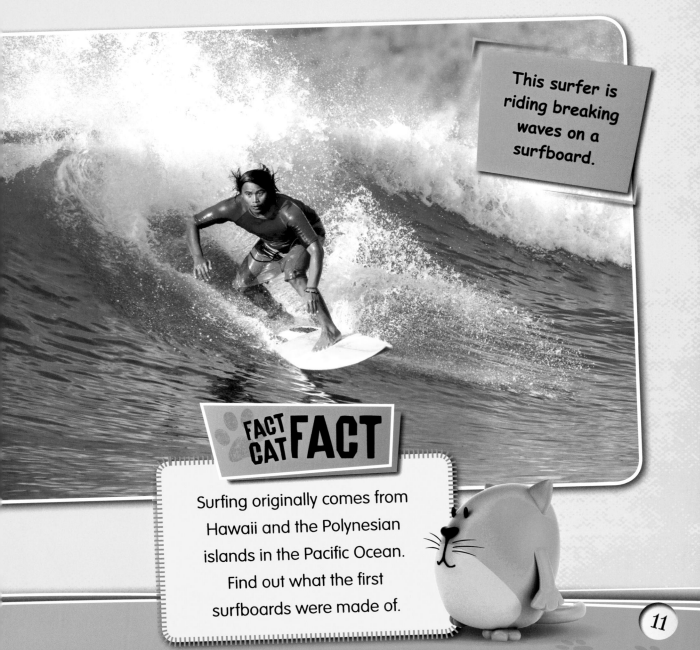

This surfer is riding breaking waves on a surfboard.

FACT CAT FACT

Surfing originally comes from Hawaii and the Polynesian islands in the Pacific Ocean. Find out what the first surfboards were made of.

THE OCEAN FLOOR

The bottom of the ocean is called the ocean floor. Near the coast, the ocean isn't very deep. The ocean floor is only a few hundred metres from the surface.

Some ocean plants and animals live in **shipwrecks** on the ocean floor.

shipwreck

In the middle of the ocean, the ocean floor can be thousands of metres from the surface. It is so **deep** that sunlight can't reach it, so this part of the ocean is very dark and cold.

This phantom anglerfish lives close to the ocean floor, in deep parts of the Atlantic and Southern Oceans.

FACT CAT FACT

The Mariana Trench is the deepest point in the ocean. It is more than 11 kilometres deep. Find out which ocean the Mariana Trench is in.

TROPICAL SEAS

Tropical **seas** are found near the **equator**. The water there is warm, and often home to **coral reefs**.

The Great Barrier Reef is the largest coral reef in the world. Find out which sea it is found in.

The Arabian Sea and the Red Sea are tropical seas in the Indian Ocean. People visit the coastlines of these two seas to go swimming and snorkelling.

Sharm el-Sheikh is a city on the Egyptian coast of the Red Sea. Its beaches are very popular with **tourists**.

FACT CAT FACT

The Red Sea is one of the saltiest seas in the world.

POLAR SEAS

The seas around the **North Pole** and the **South Pole** are called **polar seas**. They are the coldest seas on Earth, and are covered in ice for most of the year.

Icebergs sometimes break away from the ice on the water's surface. They can be dangerous to ships. Find out the name of the ship that was sunk by an iceberg in 1912.

FACT CAT FACT

Only a very small part of an iceberg is above the water. Most of it is hidden underwater.

On top of the ice, the temperature is around -60 °C. It is much warmer underwater, with temperatures of between -2 and 10 °C.

White whales, or belugas, live near the coasts of polar seas in the Arctic Ocean.

TEMPERATE SEAS

Temperate seas are found between polar and tropical seas. They are warm in some places and cold in others.

Puffins build their nests on the coastlines of temperate seas, such as the Norwegian Sea. Find a country in which people eat puffins.

The UK is **surrounded** by four temperate seas: the North Sea, the Irish Sea, the Celtic Sea and the English Channel.

FACT CAT FACT

The English Channel is only 32 kilometres wide at its **narrowest** point, so sometimes people swim across it. The fastest time anyone has swum across the Channel in is 7 hours.

Every year, more than 3.6 million **passengers** travel across the Irish Sea by **ferry**.

HOW WE USE THE OCEAN

Most of the fish that we eat is caught in **nets** by fishermen on large fishing boats.

This fisherman is taking fish out of a net by hand. On large boats, machines are used to do this job.

FACT CAT FACT

More than 77 billion kilograms of fish and shellfish are caught from the ocean every year. This is the same weight as nearly 13 million elephants!

Fuels, such as oil and gas, **form naturally** under the ocean floor. When fuels are burned, they make energy that powers cars and heats buildings.

We can collect oil and gas using giant oil rigs. This oil rig is in the North Sea. Find out which ocean the North Sea is in.

QUIZ

Try to answer the questions below. Look back through the book to help you. Check your answers on page 24.

1 How many oceans are there on Earth?

a) 6
b) 5
c) 8

2 An ocean is part of a sea. True or not true?

a) true
b) not true

3 Which country does surfing come from?

a) South Africa
b) Australia
c) Hawaii and the Polynesian islands

4 Which ocean is the Arabian Sea in?

a) The Indian Ocean
b) The Southern Ocean
c) The Atlantic Ocean

5 Most of an iceberg is above the water. True or not true?

a) true
b) not true

6 Oil and gas are found under the ocean floor. True or not true?

a) true
b) not true

GLOSSARY

billion one thousand million (1,000,000,000)

break when a wave reaches its highest point before falling forwards into the ocean

cliff high, steep rocks that form a coast

coral a hard material made by a very small sea animal

coral reef a tropical sea habitat made from coral

damage to harm something

deep when the top and the bottom of something are far apart

equator an imaginary line around the middle of the Earth

ferry a ship that regularly carries passengers across water

form to make or create

fresh water water with no salt in it

fuel something we burn to make power or heat

habitat the area where an animal or a plant lives

iceberg a large piece of ice in the ocean

million one thousand thousand (1,000,000)

narrow something with a small distance between its two sides

naturally when something happens as part of nature, and is not created by humans

net a material made of crossed threads

North Pole the most northern point on Earth

passenger someone who is travelling in a vehicle, but not driving it

pebble a small stone

polar sea a sea located near the North or the South Pole, with temperatures of between -2 and 10 °C

salt water water that contains salt

shallow when the top and the bottom of something are close together

shipwreck a damaged ship that has sunk to the ocean floor

South Pole the most southern point on Earth

surface the top part of something

surround to be entirely around something

temperate sea a sea located between polar and tropical seas, with temperatures of between 10 and 20 °C

tourist someone who visits a place on holiday and doesn't live there

tropical sea a sea located near to the equator, with temperatures of between 20 and 28 °C

INDEX

ANSWERS

Pages 4-20

Page 4: The Arctic Ocean

Page 7: Some examples include the Gulf of Mexico and the Bay of Bengal

Page 9: Canada

Page 11: Wood

Page 13: The Pacific Ocean

Page 14: The Coral Sea

Page 16: *The Titanic*

Page 18: Iceland or the Faroe Islands

Page 21: The Atlantic Ocean

Quiz answers

1 b)   5

2 b)   not true, a sea is a part of an ocean

3 c)   Hawaii

4 a)   The Indian Ocean

5 b)   not true, most of an iceberg is hidden below the water

6 a)   true

OTHER TITLES IN THE FACT CAT SERIES...

Space

The Earth 978 0 7502 8220 8
The Moon 978 0 7502 8221 5
The Planets 978 0 7502 8222 2
The Sun 978 0 7502 8223 9

United Kingdom

England 978 0 7502 8433 2
Northern Ireland 978 0 7502 8440 0
Scotland 978 0 7502 8439 4
Wales 978 0 7502 8438 7

Countries

Brazil 978 0 7502 8213 0
France 978 0 7502 8212 3
Ghana 978 0 7502 8215 4
Italy 978 0 7502 8214 7

History

Neil Armstrong 978 0 7502 9040 1
Amelia Earhart 978 0 7502 9034 0
Christopher Columbus 978 0 7502 9031 9
The Wright Brothers 978 0 7502 9037 1

Habitats

Ocean 978 0 7502 8218 5
Rainforest 978 0 7502 8219 2
Seashore 978 0 7502 8216 1
Woodland 978 0 7502 8217 8

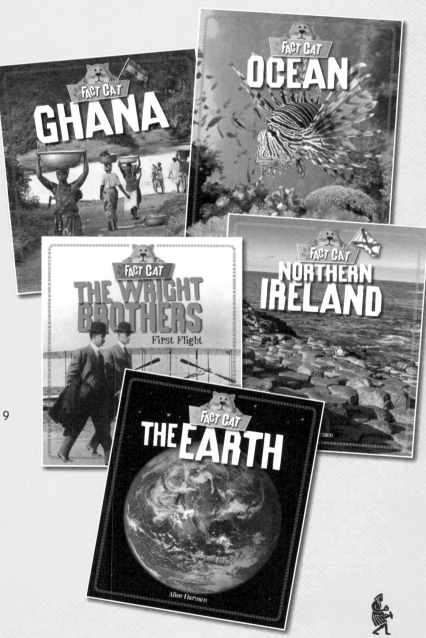

WAYLAND